Optimism Within

ONCE I

knew ONLY

darkness AND

stillness. NOW I

KNOW *hope*

AND *joy*.

Helen Keller

Optimism

WITHIN

AMERICAN ROOTS

Applewood Books
CARLISLE, MASSACHUSETTS

978-1-4290-9610-2

PUBLISHER'S NOTE

The short works Applewood includes in its
American Roots series have been selected to
connect us. The books are tactile mementos of
American passions by some of America's
most famous writers. Each of these has meant
something very personal to me.

It is unimaginable to live in a world of
darkness and no sound. When I graduated
from high school, I worked in a cerebral palsy
center, living there the rainy summer my
friends went off to Woodstock. From a wise
young supervisor, I learned that one cannot
compare the tragic circumstances of one person
to those of another. Each of us struggles with
challenges, faces them, and either overcomes
them or is overcome by them. Of all the senses I
feel blessed to possess, a sense of optimism is my
most cherished. As I grow older, it is the sense
I fight most to preserve.

*"Once I knew only darkness and
stillness. Now I know hope and joy."*

Phil Zuckerman
PUBLISHER

Could *we choose our environ-*ment, and were desire in human undertakings synonymous with endowment, all men would, I suppose, be optimists. Certainly most of us regard happiness as the proper end of all earthly enterprise. The will to be happy animates alike the philosopher, the prince and the chimney-sweep. No matter how dull, or how mean, or how wise a man is, he feels that happiness is his indisputable right.

It is curious to observe what different ideals of happiness people cherish, and in what singular places they look for this wellspring of their life. Many look for it in the hoarding of riches, some in the pride of power, and others in the achievements of art and literature; a few seek it in the exploration of their own minds, or in the search for knowledge.

Most people measure their happiness in terms of physical pleasure and material possession. Could they win some visible goal which they have set on the horizon, how happy they would be! Lacking this gift or that circumstance, they would be miserable. If happiness is to be so measured, I who cannot hear or see have every reason to sit in a corner with folded hands and weep. If I am happy in spite of my deprivations, if my happiness is so deep that it is a faith, so thoughtful that it becomes a philosophy of life,—if, in short, I am an optimist, my testimony to the creed of optimism is worth hearing. As sinners stand up in meeting and testify to the goodness of God, so one who is

called afflicted may rise up in glad-
ness of conviction and testify to
the goodness of life.

Once I knew the depth where
no hope was, and darkness lay on
the face of all things. Then love
came and set my soul free. Once I
knew only darkness and stillness.
Now I know hope and joy. Once
I fretted and beat myself against
the wall that shut me in. Now I
rejoice in the consciousness that I
can think, act and attain heaven.
My life was without past or future;
death, the pessimist would say,
"a consummation devoutly to be
wished." But a little word from

the fingers of another fell into my hand that clutched at emptiness, and my heart leaped to the rapture of living. Night fled before the day of thought, and love and joy and hope came up in a passion of obedience to knowledge. Can anyone who has escaped such captivity, who has felt the thrill and glory of freedom, be a pessimist?

My early experience was thus a leap from bad to good. If I tried, I could not check the momentum of my first leap out of the dark; to move breast forward is a habit learned suddenly at that first moment of release and rush into the light. With the first word I used intelligently, I learned to live, to think, to hope. Darkness cannot shut me in again. I have had a glimpse of the shore, and can now live by the hope of reaching it.

So my optimism is no mild and unreasoning satisfaction. A poet once said I must be happy because I did not see the bare, cold present, but lived in a beautiful dream. I do live in a beautiful dream; but that dream is the actual, the present,—not cold, but warm; not bare, but furnished with a thousand blessings. The very evil which the poet supposed would be a cruel disillusionment is necessary to the fullest knowledge of joy. Only by contact with evil could I have learned to feel by contrast the beauty of truth and love and goodness.

It is a mistake always to contemplate the good and ignore the evil, because by making people neglectful it lets in disaster. There is a dangerous optimism of ignorance and indifference. It is not enough to say that the twentieth century is the best age in the history of mankind, and to take refuge from the evils of the world in skyey dreams of good.

How many good men, prosperous and contented, looked around and saw naught but good, while millions of their fellowmen were bartered and sold like cattle! No doubt, there were comfortable optimists who thought Wilberforce a meddlesome fanatic when he was working with might and main to free the slaves. I distrust the rash optimism in this country that cries, "Hurrah, we're all right! This is the greatest nation on earth," when there are grievances that call loudly for redress. That is false optimism. Optimism that does not count the cost is like a house builded on sand. A man must understand evil and be acquainted with sorrow before he can write himself an optimist and expect others to believe that he has reason for the faith that is in him.

I know what evil is. Once or twice I have wrestled with it, and for a time felt its chilling touch on my life; so I speak with knowledge when I say that evil is of no consequence, except as a sort of mental gymnastic. For the very reason that I have come in contact with it, I am more truly an optimist. I can say with conviction that the struggle which evil necessitates is one of the greatest blessings. It makes us strong, patient, helpful men and women. It lets us into the soul of things and teaches us that although the world is full of suffering, it is full also of the overcoming of it. My optimism, then, does not rest on the absence of evil, but on a glad belief in the preponderance of good and a willing effort always to coöperate with the good, that it may prevail. I try to increase the power God has given me to see the best in everything and every one, and make that Best a part of my life. The world is sown with good; but unless I turn my glad thoughts into practical living and till my own field, I cannot reap a kernel of the good.

Thus my optimism is grounded in two worlds, myself and what is about me. I demand that the world be good, and lo, it obeys. I proclaim the world good, and facts range themselves to prove my proclamation overwhelmingly true. To what is good I open the doors of my being, and jealously shut them against what is bad. Such is the force of this beautiful and wilful conviction, it carries itself in the face of all opposition. I am never discouraged by absence of good. I never can be argued into hopelessness. Doubt and mistrust are the mere panic of timid imagination, which the steadfast heart will conquer, and the large mind transcend.

As my college days draw to a close, I find myself looking forward with beating heart and bright anticipations to what the future holds of activity for me. My share in the work of the world may be limited; but the fact that it is work makes it precious. Nay, the desire and will to work is optimism itself.

Two generations ago Carlyle flung forth his gospel of work. To the dreamers of the Revolution, who built cloud-castles of happiness, and, when the inevitable winds rent the castles asunder, turned pessimists—to those ineffectual Endymions, Alastors and Werthers, this Scots peasant, man of dreams in the hard, practical world, cried aloud his creed of labor. "Be no longer a Chaos, but a World. Produce! produce! Were it but the pitifullest infinitesimal fraction of a product, produce it, in God's name! 'Tis the utmost thou hast in thee; out with it, then. Up, up! whatsoever thy hand findeth to do, do it with thy whole might. Work while it is called To-day; for the Night cometh wherein no man may work."

Some have said Carlyle was taking refuge from a hard world by bidding men grind and toil, eyes to the earth, and so forget their misery. This is not Carlyle's thought. "Fool!" he cries, "the Ideal is in thyself; the Impediment is also in thyself. Work out the Ideal in the poor, miserable Actual; live, think, believe, and be free!" It is plain what he says, that work, production, brings life out of chaos, makes the individual a world, an order; and order is optimism.

I, too, can work, and because I love to labor with my head and my hands, I am an optimist in spite of all. I used to think I should be thwarted in my desire to do something useful. But I have found out that though the ways in which I can make myself useful are few, yet the work open to me is endless. The gladdest laborer in the vineyard may be a cripple. Even should the others outstrip him, yet the vineyard ripens in the sun each year, and the full clusters weigh into his hand. Darwin could work only half an hour at a time; yet in many diligent half-hours he laid anew the foundations of philosophy. I long to accomplish a great and noble task; but it is my chief duty and joy to accomplish humble tasks as though they were great and noble. It is my service to think how I can best fulfil the demands that each day makes upon me, and to rejoice that others can do what I cannot. Green, the historian, tells us that the world is moved along, not only by the mighty shoves of its heroes, but also by the aggregate of the tiny pushes of each honest worker; and that thought alone suffices to guide me in this dark world and wide. I love the good that others do; for their activity is an assurance that whether I can help or not, the true and the good will stand sure.

I trust, and nothing that happens disturbs my trust. I recognize the beneficence of the power which we all worship as supreme—Order, Fate, the Great Spirit, Nature, God. I recognize this power in the sun that makes all things grow and keeps life afoot. I make a friend of this indefinable force, and straightway I feel glad, brave and ready for any lot Heaven may decree for me. This is my religion of optimism.